In memory of Shari.
Happy Mother's Day 1997.
Love,
Doug & Robin

Mommy, Please Don't Cry

Tender Words for Broken Hearts

by Linda DeYmaz

illustrations by Sabrina Smith

MOMMY, PLEASE DON'T CRY
published by
Vision House Publishing
1217 NE Burnside, Suite 403
Gresham, Oregon 97030

© 1996 by Linda DeYmaz
Illustrations © 1996 by Sabrina Smith

International Standard Book Number 1-885305-45-1

96 97 98 99 00 01 02 03 04 05 - 10 9 8 7 6 5 4 3 2 1

In memory of my
precious little girl,
Alexandra
Grace
DeYmaz,
who went to be
with Jesus on
Easter morning, 1995.

This book is dedicated to mothers
everywhere who have
experienced
the deep sorrow of
losing a child.

From One Mother to Another ...

From the moment of conception, we are mothers. From the instant pregnancy is confirmed, we make plans and our dreams unfold. There is the nursery to design and wallpaper to hang; the rocker, the cradle, and the high chair to buy. We spend countless hours looking for just the right name or searching the malls for the perfect baby book. We choose the first outfit, the first toy and teddy bear. And, of course, we watch in delight and amazement as our babies and our waistlines increase!

Then, in a moment's time, our world shatters like fine china. And the darkness comes.

For some, it was a phone call from the doctor. Still others were all alone. Perhaps you found your precious baby lifeless in the crib, a heartbeat suddenly stopped. Or maybe, like me, it was in a cold, dark room that you felt life slip away as you watched a black, silent ultrasound.

Our stories are all different, but our pain is the same. We are mothers who will forever grieve the loss of our children. And yet, there is hope for our troubled souls.

It's my prayer that this simple book will satisfy your innermost longing to know that your child is wonderfully alive in Heaven. Each thought and illustration has been carefully prepared to help you feel that joy. My desire is that these words and pictures will bring a smile to your face, tears to your eyes, and great healing to your broken heart.

I will always carry a deep sorrow in the loss of my little girl. Yet in spite of this tragedy, I believe with all my heart that God sent Ali Grace to enrich my life, and to give both you and me a small glimpse of eternity.

With love,

Linda

Mommy, please
don't cry ...
A beautiful angel
carried me here!

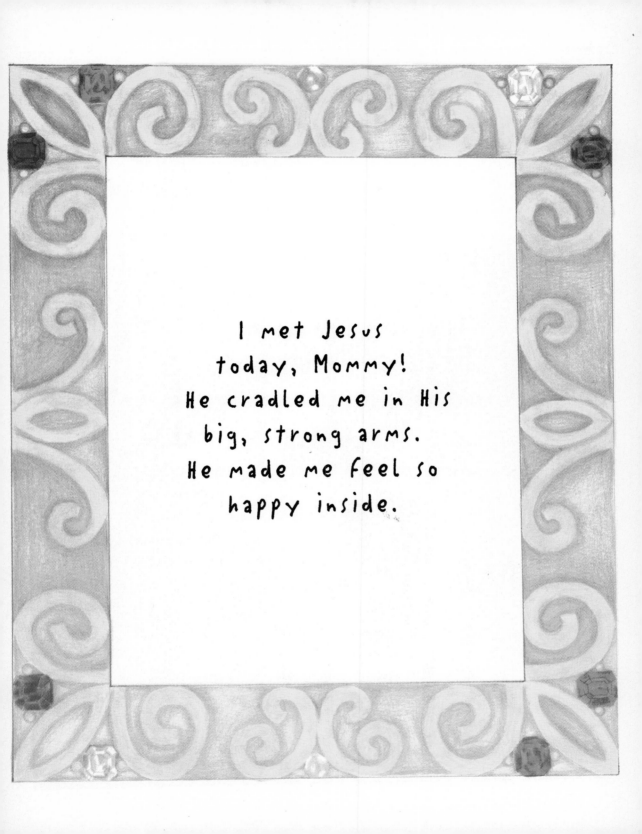

I met Jesus
today, Mommy!
He cradled me in His
big, strong arms.
He made me feel so
happy inside.

Mommy, please don't cry ...
Heaven is wonderful!
Did you know the streets
are made of gold?
Real gold!

I have lots of friends, Mommy.
We run and play, we giggle and laugh.
I can't wait to show you
my secret hideouts!

Mommy, please
don't cry ...
When I fall it
doesn't hurt!
There are no tears
in Heaven.

I've met a man named Noah.
He told me about his big boat,
all the animals, and the very first
rainbow. Have you heard
of Noah, Mommy?

Mommy, please
don't cry ...
We have lots of
parties here;
with streamers and hats,
and the best chocolate
cake ever!

When it's time to rest,
angels tuck us in.
I never get
scared Mommy,
there is no
darkness here!
Jesus is
the light of Heaven.

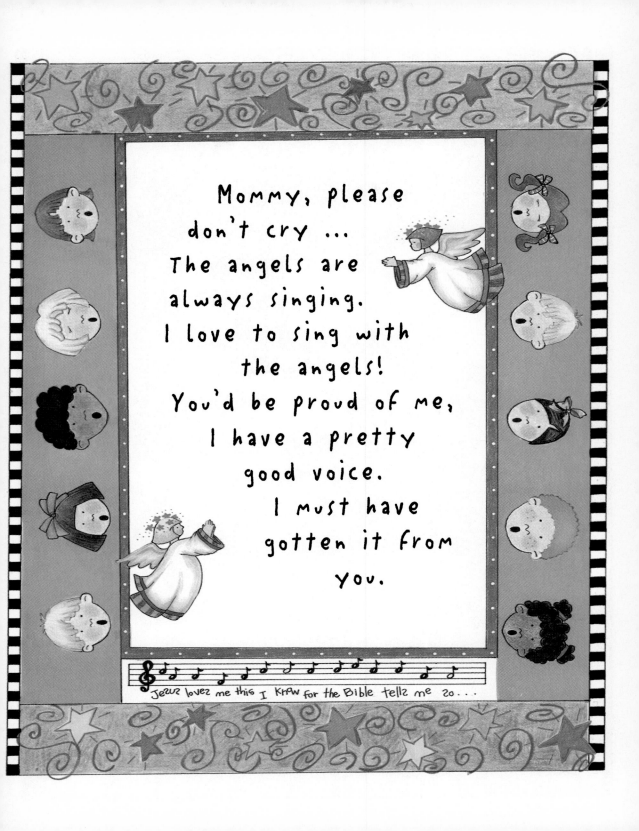

There is a river, Mommy,
in the most beautiful garden
you could ever imagine ...
and a huge tree with yummy fruit.
The angels call it the tree of Life.
Mommy, it's so wonderful
to be alive in Heaven!

Mommy, please
don't cry ...
Sometimes I just like
to be by myself.
That's when I think of you.

Someday, Mommy, we will
hold each other tight!
Then you will cradle me
in your arms,
and stroke my hair ...
And once again, our
hearts will
beat together.

Mommy, please
don't cry ...
I'll wait right
here for you.

A Bit About Heaven ...

Heaven ... is there any concept at once so inviting and at the same time so incomprehensible? There are so many questions! Where is Heaven? What's it like? Who will be there? Will we know one another? And, just what will we do there?

Although all of our questions cannot be answered now, it's surprising how specific the Bible is about Heaven. Jesus taught His followers to pray, *"Our Father in Heaven...."* From this we learn that Heaven is a real place and that God is there. The Bible also tells us that Heaven was created by God, and it is a place of light, hope, and rewards.

One of the most intriguing thoughts about Heaven is that Jesus said, *"I go to prepare a place for you."* Now, the Bible says it took God just six days to create this world–beautiful coastlines, breath-taking mountain peaks, and rolling hills. So imagine how incredible Heaven must be since Jesus has been preparing it for nearly 2000 years! Truly, *no mere man has ever seen, heard or even imagined what wonderful things God has ready for those who love the Lord.*

Throughout much of my life, the thought of Heaven intimidated me. Since I was uncertain of what it involved, I was afraid to die. However, through the experience of losing my child, I have become more intensely aware and expectant of Heaven. My deep sorrow has helped me understand the Bible and God's promises concerning Heaven.

Writing down my thoughts during quiet times of reflection helped me work through my depression and pain. For this reason, I've included a few blank pages at the back of this book if you would like to record your own special remembrances.

I often sat on my front porch and watched the beautiful sunsets, trying to envision what my little girl might be experiencing in Heaven at that very moment; running and laughing, playing with so many other little ones, walking with her great-grandparents and meeting faithful people mentioned in the Bible.

Many times my eyes have filled with tears of joy knowing that someday I will be with her again. My little child ... and yours ... are loved and cared for in that wonderful place called Heaven. They are safe and secure in the arms of Jesus.

Knowing that my little girl is alive in Heaven and that one day I will be reunited with her, is one of my deepest treasures. Heaven means more to me now and my apprehensions about death have been eased. I live with an overwhelming sense of hope and comfort, as well as with the joyful anticipation of joining her there.

You can experience this same hope and comfort if you know Jesus Christ as your Savior and Lord. All who believe in Him have eternal life in Heaven.

For God so loved the world that he gave his one and only Son,
that whoever believes in him shall not perish, but have eternal life.
John 3:16 NIV

More About Heaven ...

The Bible tells us enough about Heaven that we know it is wonderful ...
in fact, too wonderful to imagine!
The concepts in this book were taken from the following Bible verses.

*That is what is meant by the Scriptures which say
that no mere man has ever seen, heard or even imagined
what wonderful things God has ready for those who love the Lord.*
I Corinthians 2:9 LB

*And the material of the wall was jasper; and the city was pure gold, like clear glass.
The foundation stones of the city wall were adorned
with every kind of precious stone.... And the twelve gates were pearls;
each one of the gates was a single pearl.
And the street of the city was pure gold, like transparent glass.*
Revelation 21:18-19, 21 NAS

*And I heard a loud voice from the throne saying,
"Now the dwelling of God is with men, and he will live with them.
They will be his people, and God himself will be with them and be their God.
He will wipe every tear from their eyes. There will be no more death or mourning
or crying or pain, for the old order of things has passed away."*
Revelation 21:3-4 NIV

*And he showed me a river of the water of life, clear as crystal,
coming from the throne of God and of the Lamb, in the middle of its street.
And on either side of the river was the tree of life bearing twelve kinds of fruit,
yielding its fruit every month.... And there shall no longer be any night;
and they shall not have need of the light of a lamp nor the light of the sun,
because the Lord God shall illumine them;
and they shall reign forever and ever.*
Revelation 22:1-2, 5 NAS

*And they sang a new song.... Then I looked and I heard the voice of many angels
around the throne, the living creatures, and the elders;
and the number of them was ten thousand times ten thousand,
and thousands of thousands, saying with a loud voice:
"Worthy is the Lamb who was slain
To receive power and riches and wisdom,
And strength and honor and glory and blessing!"*
Revelation 5:9, 11-12 NKJ

*[Jesus] said to them, "Let the little children come to me, and do not hinder them,
for the kingdom of God belongs to such as these."*
Mark 10:14 NIV

*Take heed that you do not despise one of these little ones,
for I say to you that in heaven their angels always see the face of My Father
who is in heaven.*
Matthew 18:10 NKJ

*Finally the beggar died and was carried by the angels to be with Abraham
in the place of the righteous dead.*
Luke 16:22 LB

*Or take another illustration: A woman has ten valuable silver coins and loses one.
Won't she light a lamp and look in every corner of the house and sweep every nook
and cranny until she finds it? And then won't she call in her friends and neighbors
to rejoice with her? In the same way there is joy in the presence of the angels of
God when one sinner repents.*
Luke 15:8-10 LB

Note: *The Lamb* is a name used for Jesus Christ.

My Thoughts ...

My Thoughts ...

My Thoughts ...